Our Hands Remember

Recovering Sanikiluaq Basket Sewing

by Margaret Lawrence

Published by Inhabit Media Inc.
www.inhabitmedia.com

Inhabit Media Inc. (Iqaluit), P.O. Box 11125, Iqaluit, Nunavut, X0A 1H0
(Toronto), 191 Eglinton Avenue East, Suite 301, Toronto, Ontario, M4P 1K1

Illustrations: ivigak plant, page 24, scraping board and ulu, page 30, dehairing tool page 31 by Emma Penderson
Photographs: page 6: © Chris McNeave, page 11: © Unknown, page 13: © Annie Kavik Jr., page 14: © Margaret Lawrence,
page 18: © Margaret Lawrence, page 20: © Margaret Lawrence, page 22: © Margaret Lawrence, page 30: © Margaret Lawrence

Editors: Neil Christopher, Kelly Ward, Danielle Webster
Art Director: Danny Christopher
Designer: Astrid Arijanto

Cover photo by: Danny Christopher
Cover design by: Danny Christopher and Astrid Arijanto

Text permission: Tookoome, Simon, with Sheldon Oberman. *The Shaman's Nephew: A Life in the Far North*, 54. Toronto: Stoddart Kids, 1999. (page 9).

We acknowledge the support of the Canada Council for the Arts for our publishing program.
This project was made possible in part by the Government of Canada.

ISBN: 978-1-77227-164-5

Printed in Canada.

Library and Archives Canada Cataloguing in Publication.

Lawrence, Margaret, 1951-, author
      Our hands remember : recovering Sanikiluaq basket sewing / by
Margaret Lawrence.

ISBN 978-1-77227-164-5 (softcover)

      1. Baskets–Nunavut–Sanikiluaq. 2. Inuit–Material culture–
Nunavut–Sanikiluaq. 3. Sewing. I. Title.

TT879.B3L39 2018   746.41'2   C2018-902939-0

Table of Contents

Acknowledgements

Our Hands Remember exists because of these Sanikiluaq women: Sarah Suvvaki Kavik Appaqaq, Annie Amitook, Annie Emikotailuk Arragutainaq (now Annie Appaqaq Sr.), Minnie Kumarluk Arragutainaq, Annie Uttuqi Meeko Cookie, Bessie Saumitnaaq Crow, Annie Iqaluk Jr., Annie Kavik Jr., Hannah Arragutainaq Kavik, Sarah Suvvaki Kittosuk, Maria Appaqaq Kudluarok, Caroline Paulossie Meeko, Leah Meeko, Sarah Takatak Mickiyuk, Mary Mickiyuk, Annie Sala Novalinga, Elizabeth Kudluarok Novalinga, Emily Fleming Novalinga, Annie Tookalook, Caroline Tookalook Sr., Caroline Tookalook Jr., Annie Novalinga Qavvik, Susie Tooktoo (now Susie Eyaituk), Maggie Sala, and Rhoda Sala.

Their commitment to recover basket sewing practised for generations on the islands was supported by these people and organizations: Hamlet of Sanikiluaq and Miriam Fleming, Hamlet economic development officer; the Government of the Northwest Territories and the Government of Nunavut's Department of Economic Development and Transportation, and Culture Development Officer Eva Adams Klassen; Kakivak Association and student training funding officer Susan Gardener; Nunavut Arctic College's Fine Arts and Crafts successive head instructors Beth Biggs and Beth Beattie; and Cindy Cowan, not only for her work as Nunavut Arctic College's Coordinator of Community Programmes, but for her case study "Recovering the Traditional Art of Sanikiluaq Basket-Making," in which a group interview with Sanikiluaq women inspired the title of this book.

Community Programing provided our adult education "office" managers Shelley West, Kris Hodyr, and Johnassie Emikotailuk.

During the second year of basket sewing, Nunavut Arctic College's Fine Arts and Crafts sent Suzanne Swannie, Halifax fibre artist, and Terry Rainiger, Ontario basket weaver, to explore other fibre and basketry materials and techniques.

Also in Sanikiluaq, Qammaq Housing Association's Art Lebsack and Archie Thomas; Dwayne Searle at Mitiq Co-operative; John and Margaret Jamieson, Nuiyak School, and Fred Coman at Coman Arctic Ltd. gallery in Iqaluit had enthusiastic interest and support for the basket makers.

It took many hours for the women to visit elders, asking those who had memories to share about basket sewing in the past. These elders included one of the last doll makers, Mina Mannuk. She and Johnassie Mannuk, Mina Inuktaluk, Thomassie Kowcharlie, Sarah Kittosuk Sr. and Charlie Kittosuk, and Emily Takatak were patient and welcoming.

Inhabit Media's Neil and Danny Christopher, Kelly Ward, and Danielle Webster accepted and nurtured the idea from stories and drawings into the book in front of you. *Nakurmiimarialu*, much thanks, to all. The basket makers "volunteered" me to turn their work into this book. Any person or organization not acknowledged, and any omissions or errors are my responsibility.

To Sanikiluaq adults, Nuiyak School students, and our children who came by daily to the one-room adult-ed building: the lemmings and berries, and the encouraging warmth you brought for each step in recovering basket sewing skills and language was strengthening.

I became a different teacher through joining the women on that tarp-covered floor as a learner sharing in the challenges and pleasure of transforming *ivigak* (grass) and *qisiq* (dehaired sealskin) into baskets. To have been with them during the journey that they travelled in reclaiming their tradition taught me much more than respect for material and skill.

Although there has been no written record of early basket sewing identified with the islanders, baskets from South Baffin Inuit were collected by British and American whalers and explorers in the early nineteenth century. This book is just one part of ivigak's long history, from *Qikiqtait*, the Belcher Islands.

To heal and to create affirms how we never stop learning. We all have something to teach one another. *Sanikiluarmiut ivigaliuqtinginnut nakurmiimarialu*, to Sanikiluaq basket makers, my great thanks.

Introduction

Our Hands Remember is an important guide to traditional grass basket sewing, rich with details capturing the complex patterns and close stitching unique to the Belcher Islands. This book has enormous value in expanding our knowledge and the ability of subsequent generations to participate in this cultural practice. However, for me, and perhaps for others, the power of the story lies in the research and learning processes employed by the educator and participants to relearn something culturally significant but lost from the community. *Our Hands Remember* presents an alternative possibility for learning as it captures the sacred relationship the women have with the land, the community, and textile art. As you read, imagine gathering ivigak in the bitter winter cold and biting off the green and juicy ends of new shoots, found buried beneath the snow, to taste the approaching spring.

As Coordinator of Community Programmes, South Baffin, for Nunavut Arctic College, I made supervisory visits twice a year to communities. I joined the Sanikiluaq basket sewing project in year three, so it was well underway by the time I became involved both professionally and personally. At that time, I was struck by the peace, laughter, enthusiasm, and friendship between the women and Margaret. The uniqueness and beauty of the baskets was captivating, but as I sat and listened, seated in a circle on the floor, while the women coiled, I became fascinated by how the women wove together research and learning as they rediscovered the art of grass basket sewing. In the following two years, the Sanikiluaq project became the subject of my research during my master's degree.

One basket in particular captivated me above many others. (And there were many I fell in love with!) On the lid, serving as a handle, a soapstone carving depicts a woman sewing a *kamik* (a sealskin or caribou-skin boot). In the pouch of the *amauti* (a woman's parka with a pouch for carrying a baby), a child observes the mother. This highly representative carving adds to the beauty of the superbly crafted basket. In grass and stone, the artist brings to life the informal organic learning process that once occurred naturally as part of a traditional lifestyle. The carving depicts a "reawakening" of the memories of the child looking over her mother's shoulder while snuggled in her parka. It was through the process of gathering bits of knowledge and practising with bleeding fingers, frustration, and patience, that the women's "fingers started to remember" a shared cultural knowledge. This idea of learning and teaching illustrates a learning process that is more than a simple knowledge transfer between a teacher who is an expert and students who are empty vessels. The learning process is a collective experience of rediscovery.

Respected Inuit elder and artist Simon Tookoome has observed:

> "When I draw pictures, I think of the way it used to be when my people, the Inuit, still lived on the land. I think of legends. I think of my family at that time. I think of the shamans and I hear my uncle speaking to me in my mind."
> —Simon Tookoome, *The Shaman's Nephew*

Such reflections suggest a unity in learning, identity, and spirituality, a unity achieved through practising traditional art forms and working with the environment. Today, women weave traditional grass baskets with their memories of mothers and grandmothers; others illustrate sacred relationships. Beside them are young people, as this book attests, observing, renewing relationships, appreciating the richness of their culture and learning through dialogue, community participation, and memory. Inuit knowledge is a respected and essential foundation. *Our Hands Remember* suggests very strongly how educators and community members alike might respond to the challenges and joys of recovering traditional knowledge.

Congratulations to Margaret Lawrence, the women artists of Sanikiluaq, and Inhabit Media.

Alianait!

Cindy Cowan

Ottawa 2018

Sanikiluaq as seen from above.

Reviving Basket Sewing in Sanikiluaq

In 1988, Sanikiluaq's only school at the time, Nuiyak School, added grade ten to their previously kindergarten–to–grade nine program. I moved to Sanikiluaq, which at the time was still part of the Northwest Territories, and started my first teaching assignment there in early August of that year. The students—aged fourteen to twenty-four—and I worked together in subjects ranging from English and social studies to physical education and visual art.

The school foyer and halls displayed community artifacts and reproductions—including maps, tools, photographs, and carvings—as well as students' artwork and writing. In this visually enriched place there were also mats. Larger mats were labelled for sleeping, smaller mats for standing on while *aglu* hunting (hunting at seal breathing holes) or fish jigging out on the ice. These mats were woven from dried long grass bundles, or bundled dwarf Arctic birch, willows, or blueberry branches.

One afternoon, I went to a part of the school known as the skinroom—a room where animals were brought in, hides, furs, and meat processed, eiderdown cleaned, etc.—which also happened to be a convivial eating place. There I found the grade-ten women with elder Mina Inuktaluk, our Inuktitut and sewing teacher. Mina and the students were sitting on a tarp on the floor. They were surrounded by tied bundles of long, dried grass called *ivigak* (lyme grass). I had seen this grass on the shore and in the mats displayed throughout the school. I recognized the grass as the same species that I had found growing on the land when I worked on Baffin Island as a field assistant for plant ecologists and archeologists in the early 1980s; during those years I had often gathered willow and berry roots and spent nights weaving miniature root and twig woven baskets. The grade-ten women were quietly sewing wet grass around the dry bundles in finely-formed tight, flat coils. I was told they were making basket bottoms only, as there was only time to learn this portion.

I learned that coiled ivigak sewing was once a traditional skill for Sanikiluaq women, with a deep history in the community. Baskets were considered to be special possessions, not only because of the time and skill they took to complete, but because of the valued items they kept safe. Traditionally, baskets were made to store women's articles—sewing tools, needle case, *ivalu* (sinew thread), or anything small and easily misplaced in camp life. Yet despite this history, at the time there were no baskets being sold in the co-op store, and I did not witness anyone in our community actively pursuing basket sewing. It seemed that ivigak sewing had become a disregarded art form—along with doll-making and other types of sewing—when stone carvings became the most marketable form of Inuit art to the southern market.

After that initial introduction to ivigak sewing, I encountered infrequent examples in the community throughout the 1990s. Community member Annie Cookie brought in an old, black-and-white Polaroid snapshot of her grandmother and grandfather, Caroline and Lucassie Meeko, in their tent sometime in the early years of settlement. Her grandmother was sitting on a mattress, along with a number of ivigak baskets. Some had lids, whether topped with small bone or antler knobs or left bare. Her grandmother became blind later in life, but she continued to make and sell baskets, while many others had turned exclusively to carving. It seemed Annie's grandmother had been one of the last traditional basket makers in the community.

Then, in 1996, Nunavut Arctic College began new community programming that included a third-party funded women's sewing project designed to cater to an unseen potential consumer market for Inuit sewn goods, such as eiderdown-filled coats, vests, blankets, and pants. I became involved in this program as an instructor.

Unfortunately, the program had logistical problems. We were originally equipped with huge sewing machines that were set up for straight stitch only and could not accommodate curves or zippers. Many of the women brought machines from home to sew the clothing samples, but a number of their machines were non-electric, using hand cranks for power. The building we were working in had inadequate lighting and poor ventilation. And the new industrial sewing machines purchased for the program were held up at the airport and were frozen solid when they were finally delivered to the classroom. We took turns removing the ice and slowly going through internal machine parts to make sure they were clean and dry. It was a long and time-consuming process. Unlike portable sewing machines, each of these industrial machines had a metal pan under its base for holding oil in reserve. Even after several days of thawing, the oil in the pans was still like congealed, semi-solid lard.

We were supposed to begin sewing on the industrial machines as soon as possible, but with the machines still drying and the oil thawing, the women worried about continued funding. They received bi-weekly funding from Kakivak Association's employment training that supported participation in Nunavut Arctic College's program. For them, education and wage employment had been unavailable or limited. Others had young families depending on them. This funding made a difference for the women. We sat in a circle and talked, trying to come up with a solution for moving forward.

Group member Sarah Suvvaki Kavik Appaqaq, whose extensive skill set included carving and formal camp cook training, brought up that she and I had talked about baskets months before. She had tried to sew a basket start, the bottom of a new basket, while summer camping, with ivigak she had gathered herself. She was interested in continuing to sew with grass, although she had not been satisfied with the result of her own attempt and was unsure of how to continue. Sarah suggested that perhaps we should shift the focus of the program, at least for a short time, to learning how to make sewn ivigak baskets. The group enthusiastically accepted the idea, even though no one knew the complete process for making baskets at the outset. The

details of the skill seemed to have been lost to time, but we were eager to recover this traditional knowledge.

After explaining to Paul Taylor, the Coordinator of Community Programmes, South Baffin project supervisor, that the sewing work was delayed, the women asked for a few days to try making baskets. It was agreed that the women's sewing project would continue with sample sewing on home machines while the women set up and became accustomed to the industrial machinery. We also had permission to begin basket sewing as the women had hoped.

So, dressed warmly, with backpacks holding bannock and flasks of hot tea, we travelled by snowmobile and *qamutiik* (sled) toward the shore of Coats Bay, where ivigak grows thick around some old collapsed *qarmait* (sod houses). It was winter—not ideal for picking grass—and some of the women, myself included, were far less experienced with ivigak, but our willingness to continue was strong and we gathered what we needed to begin.

Back in the community learning centre, we laid the ivigak bundles out on a tarp overnight to dry. Soon the room began to smell like summer. We sorted and resorted the bundles, and these bundles were then divided among the women. What impressed me was that no one claimed expertise; only a

Sarah Suvvaki Kavik Appaqaq works on a basket in the community learning centre.

11

few women spoke of observing older women sewing baskets. Gradually, I realized that to work with the women as their instructor meant learning how ivigak could be made into a basket alongside them, as every aspect of the process was discussed and worked out together.

It requires patience, perseverance, and will to make baskets. With the absence of an available knowledgeable elder for guidance, the supportive and collaborative way the women of Sanikiluaq approached basket sewing was essential. The process of relearning how to make ivigak baskets was an exercise in piecing together the different bits of knowledge that each woman had. As our fingers developed calluses, we spent days talking and working out the process as a group, renewing memories, and reattaching meaning to the materials. The resources used to make the baskets were familiar—after all, a coiled basket begins in exactly the same way as sewing a circular grass table mat, something that was still done in the community—but there are unique ways to handle these resources depending on the item being created. In all stages, there was a lot of sharing among the group about how the baskets were forming—a basket could change completely as the stitches went along. For some of the women, the skill of basket sewing came back to them from where it had retreated in their memories. For others, like me, this was our introduction.

We admitted that sewing ivigak was almost habit-forming, one hand stitching while the coil in the other hand forms a curve. Stopping sometimes to feel the fine ridges of the grass threaded around the coil was a pleasant sensation, like stroking to settle fur while sewing clothing.

Through the enthusiasm and determination of the women to revive the lost skill of basket sewing, the techniques used in our class quickly evolved. After a week, some of the women admitted to sewing ivigak late at night, in any spare time they could find. The first baskets were small, but we agreed these had the form and technique of baskets. Reducing the diameter to complete the basket's lower part took more

Top: Annie Novalinga Qavvik works on a basket embellished with strips of qisiq.
Bottom: Annie Iqaluk Jr. works with ivigak.

Bessie Saumitnaaq Crow holds a basket made with qisiq strips that spell out part of a Biblical verse in Inuktitut syllabics.

discussion and practice. Sewing the coiled lid to slightly overlap the basket, while creating a tightly fitting lip to hold both parts securely, meant much trial and error. It took maybe five or six weeks, a few hours of sewing per day at the college and then at home each week, to complete those first baskets.

We quickly progressed from using un-split, whole blades of grass for stitches to the more delicate technique of splitting the grass multiple times to make a finer stitch. The women wanted to use narrow strips of qisiq to create alternating patterns with the ivigak, just as the Sanikiluaq women had used long ago. Qisiq, too, was prepared in turns and divided between all in the group. The qisiq was time-consuming to prepare and took extra care to sew flat, with the dark side out on the coil.

As the women became more comfortable with the technique, they began testing out different embellishments. Some experimented with the old way of adding colour, by dying the ivigak with berries, rather than using qisiq. Some used coloured linen weaving thread, cotton embroidery floss, and coloured, waxed artificial (nylon) sinew. Elaborate patterning emerged, with some of the women even working Inuktitut or English words into their coils. As most of the women had experience carving soapstone, bone, or antler, there also developed a variety of people- or animal-themed carvings to attach to the lids of the baskets.

This evolution developed into a style that makes baskets from our community different from Inuit baskets created elsewhere. For example, in Alaska, dyed strips of sea-mammal intestine are often used. In older Nunavik baskets, thin strips of fabric form patterns. *Nunatsiavut* baskets, sewn baskets from Newfoundland and Labrador, have distinctive scalloped or wavy, almost lace-like, borders or interstices between connected coils of ivigak. Sanikiluaq basket makers chose to sew very thin and narrow strips of dark qisiq to recall the materials used in the past. Just as carvings from different regions carry different characteristics of stone and style, so too the ivigak baskets made in Sanikiluaq carry specific markers of place and climate, from the colour and texture of the grass to the patterns selected to embellish baskets.

Perhaps one of the most valuable aspect of this whole experience, for me, was the lasting connection it encouraged. The collaborative environment created while we recovered the knowledge of sewing ivigak baskets made me look at teaching in a far less teacher-directed way, one that is most relevant to my students, and it is a perspective I continue to use in my teachings today. As we worked together on the baskets, learning and relearning from each other, we got to know one another, strengthening our community bonds. The baskets created are representative of this connection of community.

In early spring, Arts and Crafts Development Officer Eva Adams Klassen visited us to talk about the women's baskets. She wanted to take all of the women's baskets to display in a territorial trade show in Iqaluit, which several of the women agreed to. Some, however, wanted to give their first baskets to family, or to the person who had named or clothed them in infancy.

After the trade show, the basket makers asked how to get a decent price, something better than the very small amount they sold for years ago at the Hudson's Bay Company post in Great Whale River and in Sanikiluaq. While artisans and buyers were well-informed about the valuation of carvings, the decades-old information about basket sales was not satisfactory. The retail market markup system was an unknown, and it was uncertain whether the baskets would be recognized in the art community as the skills and tradition were being renewed.

But Eva was enthusiastic about the women's work, leading to supportive contacts in the territory. She was determined to help the women develop basket sewing and find fair prices for the baskets they wanted to sell.

Since the close of our sewing program in 1999, many women in the community have continued to sew baskets and have found an audience in the southern art market for their work. Baskets have since become a part of the permanent displays at Nunavut Arctic College's main campus and in the Legislative Assembly. Women took their baskets out when travelling, confident to ask for a fairer selling price; Sarah Appaqaq and Annie Cookie were invited to artists' workshops in southern Canada, the United States, and Nunavut as basket makers. Basket sewing is showing up again within the community, and people seem to be more conscious of it.

Other elders and women in Sanikiluaq began making ivigak baskets. Baskets made by Bessie Meeko Sr., Annie Ippak Sr., and Annie Emikotailuk have become known to basket collectors outside of Sanikiluaq. Their baskets, as well as the baskets made by the group of women who began sewing ivigak in the adult education building together, are often complexly patterned in coloured threads. Their baskets have Internet fans!

New generations are picking up the skills as well. I worked at Paatsaali School with two senior visual art students after school, who recently completed their first baskets and enthusiastically began work on sewing more. They made small lidded baskets for family—one of these women even sewed miniature basket earrings! On a long Air Inuit flight, the young woman beside me watched closely as I stitched on a bowl with ivigak and red thread, before exclaiming she

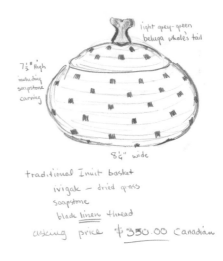

light grey-green
beluga whale's tail

7½" High
including
soapstone
carving

8½" wide

traditional Inuit basket
ivigak — dried grass
soapstone
black linen thread
asking price $350.00 Canadian

Made by Caroline Paulossie Meeko, this basket was sold through Iqaluit's Coman Arctic Gallery. Posters of each basket for sale were drawn by hand and faxed to galleries.

This basket, created by Sarah Suvvaki Kavik Appaqaq, is on display at Nunavut Arctic College in Iqaluit. The carving on the lid was made of Belcher Islands soapstone.

wanted to learn to do that, too. Then she began her own basket with that first divided blade through the coil's starting knot, stitching until her delicate coil was wider than a toonie by the time we landed in Montreal. It is heartening to see new generations eager to preserve and share this skill that had seemed lost only a couple of decades ago.

In recent years, working on illustrations, this writing, and making a qisiq-patterned basket again for Danny Christopher at Inhabit Media to photograph, I had the great pleasure to pass on what I learned with the basket makers.

Basket sewing was and is a way of remembering, of preserving Inuit cultural identity, of reaffirming connection to the people and the land. Being a part of the renewal of this traditional knowledge has been both incredibly humbling and restorative.

Basket makers young and old have ivigak in their hands again.

Where, When, and How to Collect Grass for Basket Sewing

In order to make a successful coiled basket, it is important to know the type of grass to pick, when it should be picked, and how it should be cared for. The type of grass that is used to make these baskets is known as ivigak in Inuktitut, and has several English names, one of which is lyme grass.

Where to Find Ivigak

Ivigak grows around most coastal communities in Nunavut, though the length of the grass varies, becoming shorter and less dense farther north. It is usually found growing near the seashore, a short distance from the water's edge. Ivigak is not usually found growing on sandy beaches, but some distance back from the shoreline, out of reach of high tides. At its best it grows in large, dense bunches, but it can also be found growing more sparsely in less ideal conditions. Grasses that grow inland, near freshwater lakes or rivers for instance, are not the same species of plant.

When to Collect Ivigak

Other communities have local preferences for when it is best to collect ivigak for basket sewing. These differences in timing can affect the colour of the grass that is collected. Ivigak from the Belcher Islands

has a subtle colour range that is more tan than yellow. In summer, ivigak becomes glossy and green. In autumn, it develops redness, but by spring the redness is gone from the blades. In the Belcher Islands, grass is usually collected in the spring (ideally around early May), when the snow is less hard-packed and the grass can be more easily picked. Autumn-picked ivigak is harder to sew baskets with, but it does work for woven mats.

Attempting to pick grass too early can mean that the grass will be brittle and break easily. It is best to wait until the snow has softened enough to reveal about 5–6 inches (13–15 centimetres) of grass and the stems have small exposed rings around them where the snow has melted. This extra space will allow the picker to reach down below the snow to grasp each blade separately.

No matter what time of year the grass is collected, each ivigak plant will have blades from a few years of growth to choose from. Choosing the correct blades will ensure that you have the grass you need to complete a basket.

How to Collect Ivigak

When the snow has melted enough to collect grass, head out to a patch of ivigak wearing snow pants or other waterproof pants (as you will need to kneel or bend to pick the grass), and carrying string, a few plastic shopping bags, and a backpack. There usually is no need to bring a shovel, as digging in the snow to expose the grass can actually damage the grass. Bare hands are needed to properly pick the grass, so ensure that the weather is comfortable enough to be on the land without mitts while picking. Once you arrive at an ivigak patch, and have determined that the snow has melted enough, you are ready to pick and bind ivigak.

Only the blades of the plant are usable for basket sewing, and only the blades with the best appearance should be picked. The seed stems of the plant are hollow and should not be picked. Blades closest to the centre of the plant are the current year's growth, and they will be too short to use for basket sewing. Of the outer, longer blades, you will want to pick the blades with the best appearance. A good blade of grass should have the following characteristics:

- It stands tall and is not limp and bent.
- It has a length of at least 10–18 inches (25–45 centimetres).
- It is yellower in colour (when picking in the spring) and it does not have black or brown spots.
- It has no breaks, holes, or insect bites along either side of the blade.

Be careful to only pick the blades you want to use for your basket, as you do not want to pull up an entire plant. Picking an entire plant will mean that the ivigak will not grow as thickly the following year.

When you are ready to pick the grass, kneel and reach down toward the base of the plant. Using only your thumb and forefinger, pick each individual blade using a quick, upward motion. Do not grasp the blade with your entire hand, as you may accidentally pull out more of the plant than you meant to.

Once you have gathered enough grass that the bundle fills your fist, take an older, flexible piece of grass from nearby, wrap it around the bundle, and knot it (string can also be used for this purpose if no

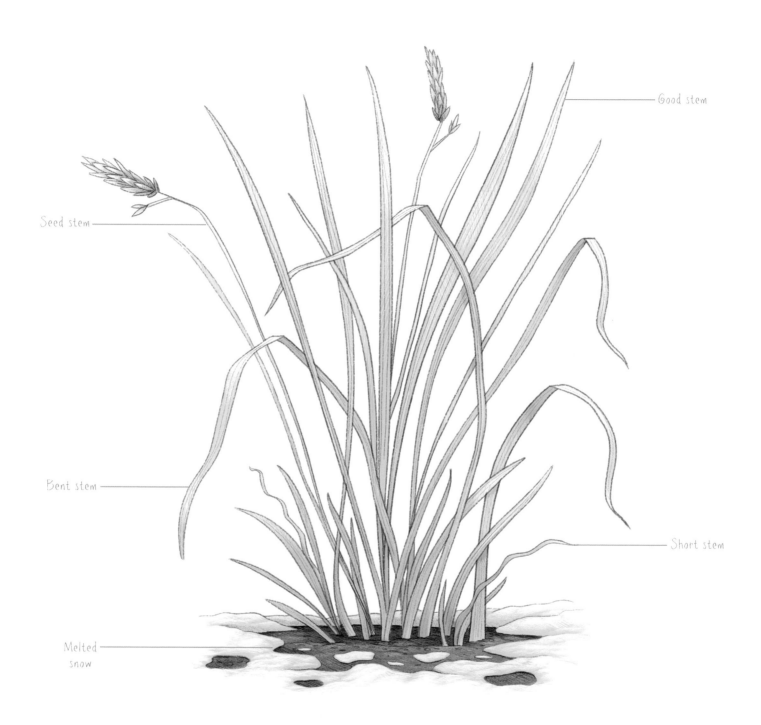

Good stem

Seed stem

Bent stem

Short stem

Melted
snow

24

suitable grass is present). Then place the bundle in a shopping bag for safekeeping while you pick the rest of your grass. If it is windy, put the bag in your backpack to ensure it does not blow away.

Pick as many bundles of ivigak as you can. If you have too much grass, you can store the grass for future use. Picking ivigak can be a time-consuming process, so make sure that you bring a snack (such as some bannock) and a thermos of tea with you for the trip. It is a pleasant activity to do with other basket makers for a few hours.

Drying and Storing Ivigak

When you arrive home, spread out an old sheet or tarp in an indoor area where it will not be bothered by foot traffic. Open each of the bundles of grass and spread the blades out so that they form a single layer on top of the sheet. It is important to spread the grass carefully in rows so that all the blades dry evenly. Sort the grass, removing any seed stocks or very damaged blades that you may have picked accidentally.

Allow the grass to dry for twenty-four to forty-eight hours. About halfway through that time, flip all the blades over. When the grass is no longer moist to the touch and feels somewhat crisp in your fingers, it is ready to be sorted and stored. The grass dries rounded, rather than opened flat.

Before storing the grass, you will need to sort it into **inside** grass (grass used for the inner coil of the basket, which is not visible on the finished basket) and **outside** grass (grass used to make the stitches of the basket itself that are visible on the finished basket).
Grass that is a bit damaged, spotty in colour, or too short (less than approximately 8 inches, or 20 centimetres) should be used as inside grass. Grass that has a good yellowish-tan colour, is free from

insect bites and other damage, and that is longer should be used as outside sewing grass.

Bundle the inside grass and outside grass separately, securing them with soft yarn or softer grass blades at each end. Do not use hard thread to secure the bundles, as this can cut the blades of grass. Package the inside grass and outside grass in separate plastic bags or pillow cases. Place these in the freezer or hang the bags in a cold porch, ensuring that there are no leaks or other water sources where you choose to store the grass. Properly dried ivigak will keep for several years, as long as it does not get wet.

Other Materials and Tools Needed for Basket Sewing

In addition to grass, there are several tools and materials you will need in order to complete a coiled basket. Qisiq—thinly cut, dehaired sealskin—is traditionally used to make the distinctive dark-brown decorative patterns on coiled baskets. While other types of embellishments can be used, such as embroidery thread, Sanikiluaq basket makers feel strongly that qisiq is a beautiful and important part of the materials used in their baskets. Bans on the sale of seal products to various countries throughout the world have meant that baskets intended for sale in the southern market are sewn without qisiq. Women making baskets for sale use manufactured cotton, hemp, linen, or waxed nylon threads for patterning. There are several tools needed to prepare the qisiq for use in a coiled basket. There are also several other tools needed to complete the basket. It is important to ensure that you have all the tools you need in order to help finish the basket.

Preparing Qisiq for Use in a Coiled Basket

Qisiq is dried and scraped skin from a ringed seal. To prepare a sealskin for use in a basket, begin by removing the skin of the seal's head, tail, and flippers, as this area of skin is not used for this purpose.

Both sides of the skin need to be scraped before the skin can be cut. To begin scraping the skin, lay it on a wooden scraping board (a board that is higher at one end to allow a good angle for scraping). Then, scrape the inside of the skin until it is clear of fat using a sharpened ulu. When scraping either the fat side or

Scraping board

Ulu

the haired side of the skin, always hold your sharpened ulu at an oblique angle (approximately 45 degrees) to ensure that you do not cut through the skin itself.

Once the inside of the skin has been scraped free of fat layers, make holes around the entire circumference of the skin. Use these holes to hang the skin on a drying rack. Drying racks are usually made from wood or metal and can be shaped as either a semi-circle (on which the skin is folded in half and hung) or an uneven hexagon (on which the skin is hung in a single layer). Thread the skin onto the drying rack and pull tightly. Ensure that the skin is left to dry somewhere out of reach of dogs, as dogs will attempt to eat drying skins. The skin is dry when it is firm to the touch.

Once the skin has been dried and the haired side has been scraped once, each side should be scraped one more time. The unhaired side should be scraped to remove any remaining dried skin flakes, ensuring the hide is as thin as possible. Making small, scalloped motions at the same 45-degree angle is the best way to remove these stubborn flakes. The haired side, now dark brown after its first scraping, should be scraped once again—against the grain of the hair, using an ulu—until the skin becomes a smoother dark brown. Even when the skin has been completely scraped, you will still be able to feel the grain of the hair follicles.

After the second round of scraping is complete, you are ready to cut the qisiq. Remove the entire thicker, outside edge of the skin where the holes for drying the skin were punched. The remaining qisiq can then be cut into thin strips for use in a coiled basket. The ideal thickness of the strips will depend on the size of the basket you are making. The larger the basket, the thicker the strips can be. Generally, strips of 2 to 3 millimetres in width work well for a medium-sized basket. An ulu can be used to cut the strips, but you may find that scissors are easier to use to ensure a very straight cut. It is imperative that the strips have the same thickness across their entire length, and that they follow the grain of the hair down the seal's body.

Along with any uncut qisiq, the strips can then be placed in a clear plastic bag and stored in the freezer. Qisiq that is stored in this way will keep for many years. Qisiq will curl a bit in the bag when it is stored, but it will return to its original shape when it is thawed.

Preparing qisiq is a very time-consuming process, so it is helpful to have a partner to help you prepare the skin. Since qisiq is only used for patterned

Dehairing tool

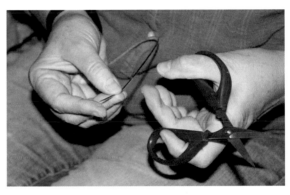

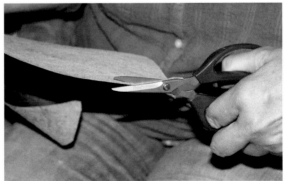

embellishments, there is usually enough qisiq from one skin for several basket makers to share.

Needles

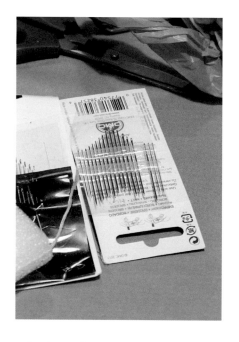

Various types of sewing needles are necessary to ensure a properly sewn basket.

For sewing with grass, use a standard sewing needle, often known as a "sharp" needle. These needles have a round eye and a sharp tip. Choose a size of sharp needle with an eye that allows you to sew the width of the ivigak blade you are using to make your particular basket. For sewing with qisiq, use an embroidery needle. These needles are longer than sharp needles and have a sharp tip and an oval-shaped eye.

Whether selecting sharp needles or embroidery needles, it is best to select good-quality steel needles, as the needles must be very strong. Sewing with grass and sealskin wears out the eyes of needles faster than sewing with thread. You will need more than one needle of each type to ensure that you have backup needles.

Thimbles

Many basket makers prefer to wear thimbles (known as *tikiq* in Inuktitut) while sewing. A thimble is a small cup-shaped finger cover that saves a sewer's finger from being pricked by needles and otherwise damaged as she sews. Thumbles can be of the store-bought, metal variety or can be made at home using a small piece of sealskin or other leather.

Pliers

Small, needle-nosed pliers are an essential tool for sewing coiled baskets. Stitches can become very tight, especially when sewing with qisiq, which is thicker than grass. Using pliers to pull the stitch through will make sewing much easier! Select the smallest pliers you can find in the needle nosed style (elongated blades with ridges on the inside edges). A spring handle makes the pliers even easier to use, but pliers without a spring can also be used.

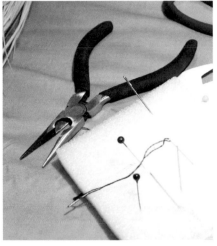

Scissors

Scissors or a small sharpened sewing ulu (an ulu of no more than 3 inches, or 8 centimetres, in diameter) are useful for cutting angled, pointed ends for inside grass, and for cutting a point in each qisiq strip to help thread it more easily through the embroidery needle. If using a sewing ulu, you will also need a sharpening rock or another ulu to ensure that you can keep your ulu sharp enough to use.

Where to Sew a Basket

Having a comfortable environment for sewing a basket is nearly as important as having the proper tools. Sitting on a well-lit, clean, clear area of floor is best. Have an open outside grass bundle nearby in a damp cloth, and keep inside grass and all the basket sewing tools close by. This also means that dropped needles do not have as far to "wander."

It takes hours of practice to develop *kaut* (callouses) on the fingers. Kaut, as well as hand and back strength, make working on baskets more comfortable and will allow you to enjoy sewing for longer periods.

Sewing a basket is a long process, but time passes enjoyably if you sew with other basket makers, or while listening to music, stories, or a local radio broadcast.

Sewing a Basket: Step-by-Step Instructions

Note: Photos are of a left-handed sewer.

The basket being created in the photographs took about two and a half outside bundles and two inside bundles of ivigak.

A miniature basket (the size of the ball of a thumb, or an eyeball) can take four to twelve hours to make; an apple-sized basket takes approximately fifteen to twenty-five hours; and a larger basket can take upward of sixty hours to complete A very large basket can take up to 100 hours to complete!

Preparing the Grass

To prepare your outside grass (wet grass), which will be used for the stitches of the basket:

- Soak the blades in cold water (warm water will promote rot spots) in a clean sink or tub for forty-five minutes to an hour. Any longer and the grass will begin to rot. Do not leave overnight!
- If the grass is floating, wash a few rocks and carefully lay them over the grass to hold the blades under the water.

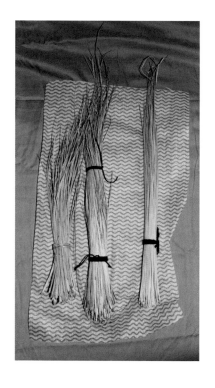

- Dampen a clean tea towel. Remove the grass from the water and roll it up in the damp tea towel. Wrap it in a plastic bag and put it in the freezer to temper the grass.
- When you are ready to work, remove the towel-wrapped grass from the freezer and defrost it for about twenty to thirty minutes.
- When you are not using the grass, always remember to put wet grass back in the freezer. If the grass is starting to dry, dampen it with water before putting it back in the freezer. Freezing seems to condition wet ivigak better than just sewing it damp. When you are ready to use it again, defrost it for about twenty to thirty minutes.

Select your bundles of inside grass (dry grass), which will be used to build up the coils of your basket. Unlike outside grass, inside grass may already be mottled or damaged—as long as it is used dry, it is still strong.

- Store dry grass in a dry, dark place until ready to use.
- Do not dampen.

Making the Thread

1. Using your fingers, unfurl a new piece of wet grass from bottom to top. The outside is smooth and shiny; the inside is rough.
2. Take a needle and run it up the blade of grass to separate it into threads. Separate the blade into three or four threads for a small basket, or two or three threads for larger baskets.

3. Keep your threads with your wet grass while you work so they do not dry out.
4. Roll each piece of thread between your thumb and forefinger so that it curls in on itself with the smooth side out.

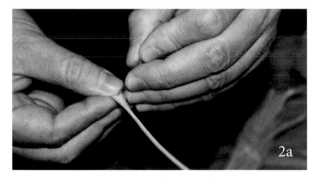

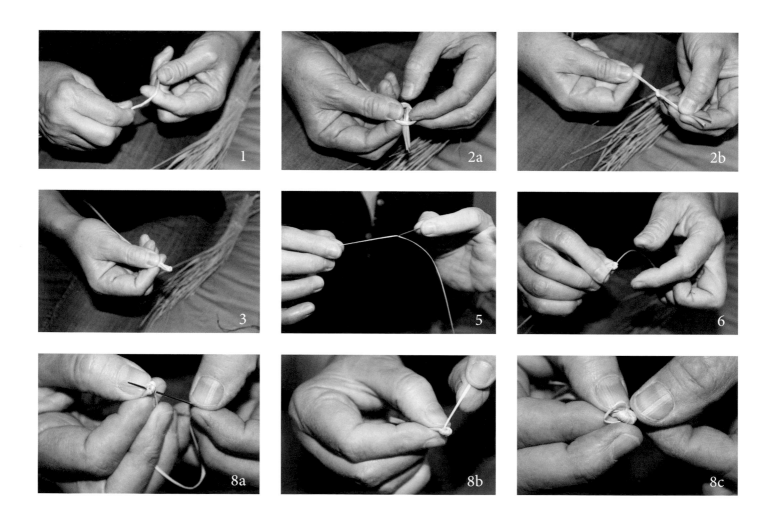

The Basket Start

The bottom of a sewn basket is known as "the basket start." It is the beginning of the coils and forms the bottom of the basket.

1. For a larger basket, start with two or three whole pieces of damp outside grass; for smaller baskets, start with one piece. Gently flex each piece back and forth with your fingers (without breaking it) to loosen the blade.

2. Tie a simple knot at the thicker end of your starting piece(s), leaving a tail about the length of your thumb. Pull the knot tight.

3. Fold the tail over into your hand so that the knot is pointing out. You want the knot to lie flat (gently bite it to flatten). The tail ends will become inside parts of the coil as sewing continues.

4. Select a sharp needle with an eye big enough that your grass thread will fit through smoothly without being forced, or else the grass could break.

5. Thread the needle with one of your outside, rolled grass threads.

6. Put the needle through the centre of the knot, leaving a tail about half a thumb-length long. Fold the tail into your hand, holding it along with the tail from the knot.

7. Note: For your basket start, it does not matter which hand you are using to control the coils and which is controlling the needle. Use whichever way feels most comfortable. Once you start to form the sides, though, you will need to commit to one hand or the other.

8. Stitch around the knot coming back through the centre each time, pulling the stitches firmly but gently. Make sure the overlapping stitches of thread lie so that the smooth side is facing outward. Keep stitching your way around the knot in a circle, gradually curving your starting piece(s) of inside grass (the grass you used to form the knot) as you work around the knot so that your stitches incorporate this grass into the coil. Each stitch should slightly overlap the previous stitch, with minimal gaps of inside grass showing.

9. Use pliers to help get the needle through the knot if it gives you a hard time.
10. After you have gone around the knot, begin catching your stitches on the outside edge of the first coil, rather than going through the centre of the knot.
11. Continue stitching around the coils, being sure to keep even pressure with your fingers on both sides of the coils so the bottom of your basket will be flat.

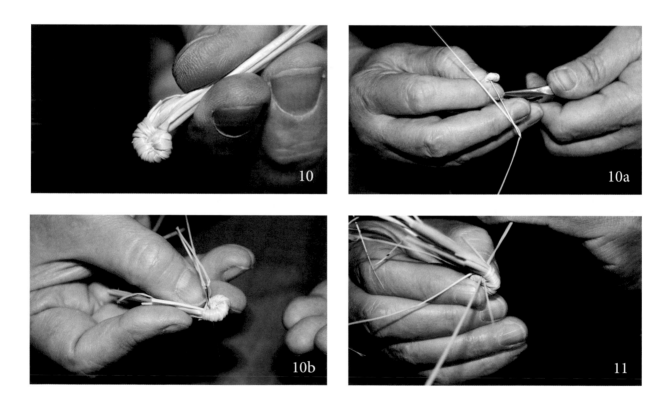

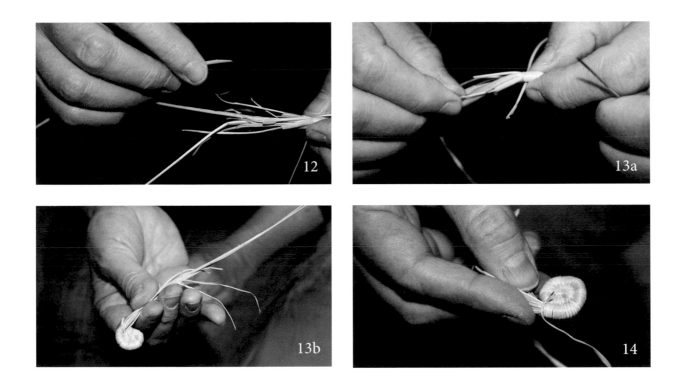

12. Take a new piece of dry inside grass and cut the root-end—the bottom of the blade is thicker—at a sharp angle.
13. Tuck the bottom of this blade into the coil when the diameter of the coil is big enough to hold it. If the dry blade keeps falling out, continue the coil without the inside grass until the diameter is large enough that the blade will not fall out when inserted into the coil.
14. Continue to stitch around these inside blades.

15. Add new pieces of inside grass one at a time at regular intervals. The grass blades are tapered, so build up the coils gradually to maintain a consistent coil size. If you build up too fast, the coils will not be even.

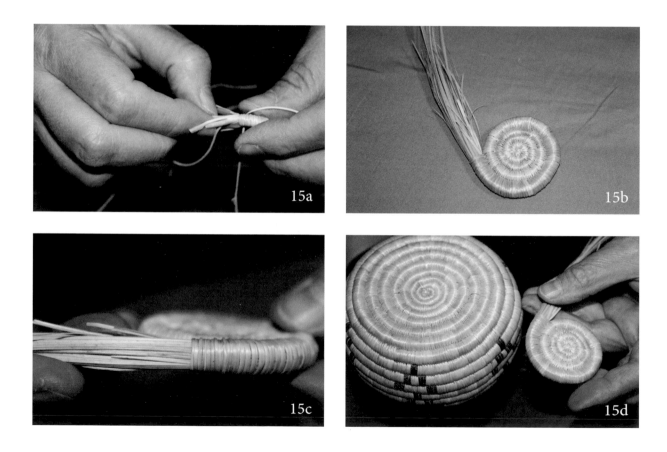

When Your Thread Runs Out or Breaks

1. Fold the exposed tail end of the thread into the coil with the rest of the inside grass.
2. Thread the needle with a new piece of rolled, damp thread of outside grass.
3. With this new piece, make a stitch slightly overlapping the last completed stitch and continue around the coil, folding the tail of each new thread into the coil as well.

Forming the Sides of a Curved Basket

1. When the basket bottom is a desirable size, begin angling your coils slightly outward by applying pressure with your thumb and forefinger to the outermost coil and catching your stitches slightly higher on the previous coil, angling your needle as well.
2. Continue around as you did the bottom, but now maintaining the angle and pressure.
3. When you reach the desired middle height, as well as diameter, of your basket, alter the pressure and angle with your fingers, and catch the stitches on the top inside edge of the previous coil so that the coils will now curve inward.

1a

1b

1c

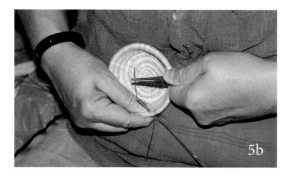

Traditional Qisiq Embellishments

1. Choose an embroidery needle with an eye opening appropriate to the size of your qisiq threads.
2. Cut an angle into one end of the qisiq thread so that the grain is going down from the needle eye.
3. Thread the qisiq through the needle about a third of the way down and fold at the eye.
4. Hold the piece of outside grass you had been working with into the coil.
5. Insert the needle so that it catches your last stitch and pull through, leaving yourself a tail of qisiq about half a thumb length.
6. Fold this tail end of the qisiq with the inside grass.
7. Stitch around the coil just as you did with the grass thread, but remember to keep the qisiq thread flat, the stitches close together, and the dark side facing outward—this may take some jiggling as the thread twists inside-out easily. You will likely want to use needle-nose pliers for this stage as it will be more difficult to stitch through the qisiq. Do not use your teeth to pull the qisiq needle through, as damage may occur.

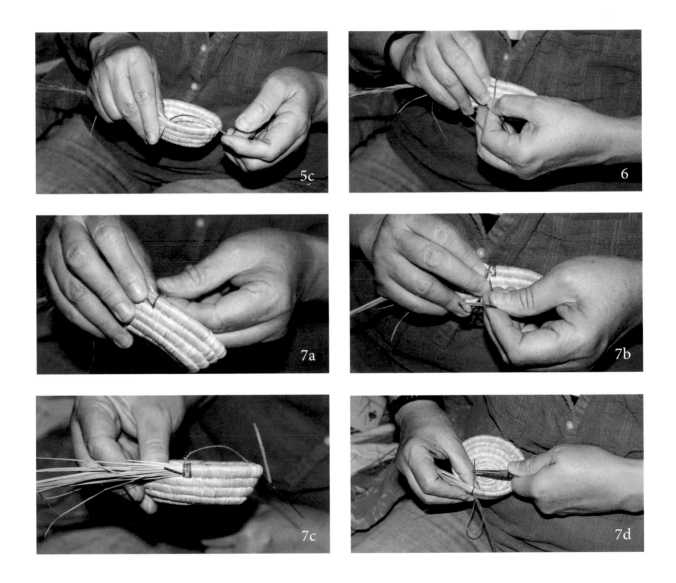

8. When done, cut off the qisiq, leaving another tail that can be held within the coil.
9. Continue stitching with outside grass, alternating with qisiq until the pattern intervals complete the circumference.
10. Store any unused qisiq threads in the freezer in a sealed plastic bag. Damp qisiq unintentionally left in a warm place may develop mold.
11. Note: Other types of embellishments, such as embroidery thread, may be used in place of qisiq.

Finishing the Last Coil

1. When your basket opening is a desirable size, cut the remaining inside grass of the coil at an angle so that the coil will become smaller and tapered as you sew.
2. Carefully continue stitching past the loose ends by several stitches to create a smooth, even finish.

1a

1b

1c

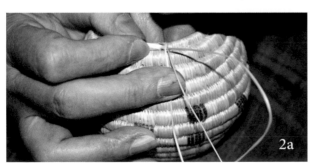

2a

2b

3. End with the thread on the inside of the basket coil and clip the ivigak thread as close to the basket's side as possible.

Tip for Creating Even Patterns

1. Cut a paper circle the same circumference as the coil you are working on.
2. Fold the circle in half four times. Cut the outside edge at an angle. When the circle is unfolded, you should have eight points. Use these points as starting points for your embellishments.
3. Holding the cutout over your basket, mark your starting points with straight pins or a fine-point pen. These marks indicate where to use your qisiq threads.

Alternate Shapes

- **Flat:** Instead of angling the sides, continue sewing around your basket start, keeping the coils flat. Finish off the last coil when the mat is the desired size. These mats are not traditional shapes, but can be used for displaying items such as baskets or dolls.
- **Bowl:** Rather than reversing the angle of the coils at the halfway point, as you would with a curved basket, create a bowl shape by finishing off the last coil at the desired bowl circumference.
- **Straight:** Rather than angling the sides as you would for a curved basket, keep your fingers and thumb straight on either side of the coil and catch the stitches through the top of the previous coil. For your last coil, angle this coil toward the inside of the basket, catching the stitches toward the inside edge rather than at the top. This will create a small inner lip to hold the lid placed on top. The rim of your lid should be the same circumference as your basket (not the last coil), rather than extending beyond the side.
- Basket bottoms can be circular or oval. This will influence the shape of the overall basket. For an oval basket start:
  - Sew the first few stitches through your starting knot as you would a circular basket, but instead of continuing around the knot again, sew outward, stitching through the tail end of your starting piece. You should have a straight piece of coil. The length of this piece will determine the length of your basket. If you make this starting piece too long you could end up with a very long, narrow basket.
  - When you reach the desired length of your starting coil, flip the inside grass back on itself.
  - Sew around the bend and then straight back toward your starting knot, catching your stitches in the side of your starting piece.
  - At the knot, curve the inside grass around the knot so that you are stitching around and straight down the opposite side of the starting coil.
  - Continue sewing around the outside in one direction until you have the desired size of your basket bottom.
  - Remember to build up the coils with inside grass as you sew, just as you would with a curved basket.

Lids

1. Baskets can be lidless, but if you want to add a lid, a sewn lid can be flat or domed. Decide which style you will be making. The style you prefer may influence the carving or topper made for the lid.
2. Start the lid the same way as your basket start. If making a flat lid, keep even pressure on both sides of the lid as you would a basket bottom. If making a domed lid, apply pressure on one side of the lid with your thumb, stitching at an angle as you form the coils to create a curve (similar to creating the sides of a curved basket).
3. Test for size. The lid should have a slightly greater circumference than the opening of your basket.

4. Finish the last coil as you would a basket opening, by cutting the inside grass on a tapering angle and then stitching past the loose ends to create a smooth finish.
5. Cut off the thread on the underside of the lid, as close to the lid as possible.
6. Using one or two threads of outside grass, stitch a whole piece of wet grass to the underside of the lid, leaving enough of a lip around the edge that this coil will fit snugly inside the basket opening.
   • Tip for Getting the Right Fit: Roll a sheet of paper into a tube and place it inside the opening of your basket. Allow the roll to unfurl to the size of your basket opening. With a small piece of tape, secure the paper roll so that it will not unfurl when removed. Now you have the perfect circumference of your basket opening. Use the end of the paper tube as a guide while stitching the first coil to the underside of your lid.*

*I give full credit for this useful technique to Annie Cookie.

7. Add in more wet grass every few stitches to build up the coil.
8. After reaching about 1 inch (3 centimetres) or so in height, start adding dry grass to the coil instead of wet.
9. Continue to build up the coils, testing for fit frequently as you go. Two or three coils in depth should be enough for a secure fit inside the basket's rim.

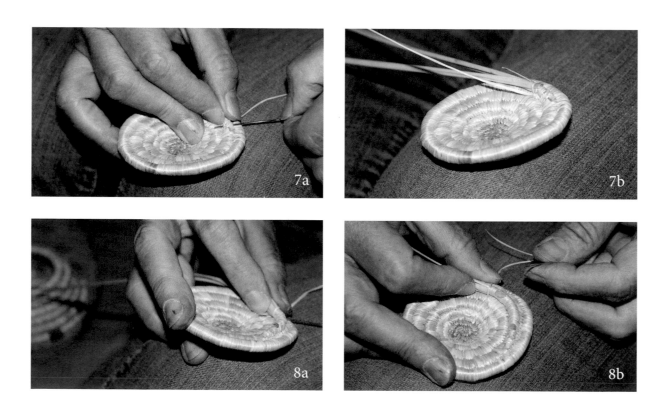

10. Finish the last coil as you would a basket edge, by cutting the inside grass at an angle and stitching past the loose ends for a smooth finish.
11. Test for fit. If the lid does not fit, save it for another basket and start a new one. Even for experienced basket makers, making a lid that fits can be a challenge.
12. You may wish to make your lid first and make a basket to fit the lid, rather than the other way around.

Lid Toppers

Lid toppers can consist of stone, antler, ivory, or bone carvings, small sewn objects, or even small rocks.

- When deciding on a topper, consider how it suits the basket in size and balance. Adornments can be sewn onto the lid using synthetic sinew.
- Traditional toppers include antler or bone knobs.
- Soapstone carvings can be sewn onto lids, as well, or even used in place of a woven lid.
- Small, sewn *kamiik* (a pair of sealskin or caribou-skin boots) or dolls may be sewn on top.

Maintenance

- Do not remove the basket lid using the topper. Always lift by gently prying around the lip of the lid. A lid that has been fitted properly requires some pressure to remove for security.
- Do not leave the basket in direct sunlight.
- Clean using a light, dry cloth.
- Do not wet the basket or it will rot.
- You should not wax or spray a basket.
- The baskets will mellow gently in colour over time, but this should not discourage use—they are meant to be handled, after all.

Additional Information

If you want to look at examples of ivigak baskets, the internet is an excellent place to start, turning up numerous search results. You may find galleries that represent particular contemporary Inuit basket makers, and museums where older baskets have become part of collections through trade, exploration, and ethnographic contact. Not every coiled basket shown will be made by Inuit, but it will become easier to identify ivigak baskets as you look carefully. For example, in Alaska, some baskets have been made from soaked baleen strips and twined fine roots—techniques and materials that differ from those used in Canadian Inuit ivigak baskets.

Should you be interested in seeing some of the oldest Canadian Inuit ivigak baskets, the British Museum in London, England, has coil-sewn baskets from whaler William Penny's time overwintering in Cumberland Sound in the 1840s. Charles Francis Hall, after exploring Frobisher Bay with Inuit in the 1860s, returned with ivigak baskets that are now in the Smithsonian in Washington, DC. And the Royal Ontario Museum in Toronto, Ontario, has a large collection of ivigak baskets from the early 1900s to about 1980 that were donated by Av Isaacs, former owner of the Isaacs Gallery of Inuit Art.

The oldest coiled basket from a Canadian High Arctic archaeological site is at the Canadian Museum of History in Gatineau, Québec. This very small container appears to have been made by coiling thin roots around an ascending, larger root coil. It has gaps and may have required a bone or ivory awl to thread the fine roots through and around. Found in the permafrost, this patinated artifact survived centuries.

Ivigak baskets made by *Sanikiluarmiut* (residents of Sanikiluaq) are showcased in permanent displays at the Legislative Assembly and the main campus of Nunavut Arctic College, both in Iqaluit, Nunavut.

Further Reading

Cowan, Cindy. "An Inquiry into Emancipatory Adult Education for Indigenous People." Thesis, St. Francis Xavier University, 2003. http://www.collectionscanada.gc.ca/obj/s4/f2/dsk4/etd/MQ77068.pdf

Craft Labrador. http://www.craftlabrador.com.

Driscoll, Bernadette, Ed Horn, Patrica Sieber, Spencer G. Sealy. *Belcher Island: Sanikiluaq.* Winnipeg: Winnipeg Art Gallery, 1981.

Hamlet of Sanikiluaq. *Municipality of Sanikiluaq.* https://www.sanikiluaq.ca/i18n/english/index.html.

Lee, Molly. "Alaska Eskimo Baskets: Types and Prototypes." In *Faces, Voices and Dreams: A Celebration of the Centennial of the Sheldon Jackson Museum Sitka, Alaska 1888–1988*, edited by Peter L. Cory. Seattle: University of Washington Press, 1987.

Lee, Molly. "Siberian Sources of Alaskan Eskimo Coiled Basketry." *American Indian Art Magazine* 20, no. 4 (Autumn 1995).

McGhee, Robert. *Ancient People of the Arctic.* Vancouver: University of British Columbia Press, 2001.

Miles, Charles, and Pierre Bovis. *American Indian and Eskimo Basketry: A Key to Identification.* New York: Bonanza Books, 1969.

Pharand, Sylvie. *Caribou Skin Clothing of the Igloolik Inuit.* Iqaluit: Inhabit Media, 2012.

Qikiqtani Inuit Association. *Qikiqtani Truth Commission Community Histories 1950–1975: Sanikiluaq.* Iqaluit: Inhabit Media, 2013.

Vorano, Norman. "Creators: Negotiating the Art World for Over 50 Years." In *Inuit Art Quarterly* 19, no. 3 & 4 (Fall/Winter 2004): 9–17.

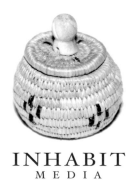

INHABIT
M E D I A